Date: 3/17/16

J 636.8 CON
Conley, Kate A.,
Burmilla cats /

Burmilla Cats

Kate Conley

Checkerboard Library
An Imprint of Abdo Publishing
abdopublishing.com

abdopublishing.com

Published by Abdo Publishing, a division of ABDO, PO Box 398166, Minneapolis, MN 55439.
Copyright © 2016 by Abdo Consulting Group, Inc. International copyrights reserved in all
countries. No part of this book may be reproduced in any form without written permission from
the publisher. Checkerboard Library™ is a trademark and logo of Abdo Publishing.

Printed in the United States of America, North Mankato, Minnesota.
042015
092015

Cover Photo: Photo by Helmi Flick
Interior Photos: Alamy p. 1; Glow Images pp. 11, 17; Photos by Helmi Flick pp. 5, 21;
    iStockphoto pp. 6, 7, 9, 15, 16; Minden Pictures pp. 13, 19

Series Coordinator: Tamara L. Britton
Editors: Tamara L. Britton, Bridget O'Brien
Art Direction: Neil Klinepier

Library of Congress Cataloging-in-Publication Data

Conley, Kate A., 1977- author.
  Burmilla cats / Kate Conley.
      pages cm. -- (Cats. Set 9)
  Includes index.
  ISBN 978-1-62403-810-5
1. Burmilla cat--Juvenile literature. 2. Cat breeds--Juvenile literature. 3. Cats--Juvenile
literature. I. Title.
  SF449.B84C66 2016
  636.8--dc23
                                         2015008836

Contents

Lions, Tigers, and Cats

The Burmilla is a cat **breed** that began in England not long ago. Though the breed is new, it belongs to an old family. Like all cats, Burmillas are part of the family **Felidae**. It includes 37 different cat species.

The members of the family Felidae share many **traits**. They are graceful hunters. They use their sharp teeth and claws for capturing prey. They are also skilled at jumping and climbing.

Cats were **domesticated** about 3,500 years ago. These early cats were used to patrol stored grains, keeping them free from mice and other pests. Today, domestic cats such as the Burmilla are beloved pets.

The Burmilla cat

Burmilla Cats

The Burmilla first appeared in England in 1981. That year, a Burmese cat named Bambino Lilac Fabergé (fah-behr-zhay) escaped from her home. She mated with a chinchilla Persian cat named Jemari Sanquist. Their kittens were the first Burmillas.

There were four females in the first Burmilla **litter**. Their coats were black and silver shaded. In this type of coat, the cat's fur is silver closest to the root. Then the hair turns black near the tip. The owners thought the cats were

so beautiful that they should continue to **breed** them.

Today, the Burmilla is an experimental breed. That means it is still being developed. The Burmilla became a **Cat Fanciers' Association** breed in 2011. However, these cats are rare outside of England.

The Burmilla cat was developed from mating the Burmese *(far left)* and Persian *(left)* breeds.

Qualities

Burmillas are known for their sweet dispositions. These cats are gentle, playful, and curious. They love spending time with their owners. Burmillas make good pets for families with young children and other animals.

The personality of a Burmilla is a mix of **traits** from its Persian and Burmese relatives. Burmillas are outgoing and friendly, just like the Burmese. Like Persians, Burmillas are relaxed and calm.

Burmillas love to have fun. They often act like kittens even when they are adults. They enjoy playing with their owners and their toys. Burmillas are also smart cats. Some have been known to use their paws to open cupboard doors and turn on faucets!

The Burmilla is loving, loyal, and affectionate.

Coat and Color

A Burmilla's coat can be long or short. Burmillas with short coats have a soft coat with fine, silky fur. It lays closely to the body. Longhair Burmillas have the same fine, silky fur but it is longer. They also have fluffy tails and **tufts** on their ears.

Burmillas are known for the color of their coats. They have a silver **undercoat**. The fur of the topcoat can be tipped or shaded. Tipped coats have color on the tip of each hair. Shaded coats have color on one-third of each hair. This type of coloring gives the Burmilla a silvery, shimmering appearance.

At first, all Burmillas had black and silver shaded coats. After years of **breeding**, the Burmilla gained a greater variety of coat colors. Today, the coat can be shaded or tipped in 13 colors. These include brown, **blue**, red, chocolate, **lilac**, and **tortoiseshell**.

This Burmilla kitten has a red shaded coat.

Size

Burmillas have wedge-shaped heads. The tips of their ears are rounded, and their **muzzles** are short. Burmillas have green eyes, though in cats less than two years old the eyes can be yellow.

Burmillas are medium-sized cats. When they are fully grown, they weigh between 8 and 10 pounds (3.5 and 4.5 kg). Burmillas are generally healthy cats. With proper care, they can live between 7 and 12 years.

Burmillas have stocky bodies. Their chests are rounded, and they have large muscles and bones. They have straight, strong backs and slim legs. The hind legs are a little longer than the front legs. The paws are small and oval.

The Burmilla's eyes, nose, and lips have a black outline.

Care

Caring for a Burmilla begins at the veterinarian. The vet will examine the cat to be sure it is healthy. If the cat has not yet received its **vaccines**, the vet can provide those. Vets can also **spay** or **neuter** cats.

At home, Burmillas also need good care. They should have a **litter box** in which to eliminate waste. It should be cleaned often. This is important, since some cats will refuse to use a dirty litter box.

The Burmilla's coat does **shed**. A good brushing each day will help keep the coat healthy. This is also a good time to trim the cat's claws and clean its ears if needed.

Burmillas like to climb and jump, so giving them a perch or cat tree is a good idea. Like other cats, Burmillas also like to scratch. It is a natural cat behavior that keeps the claws sharp. Providing a scratching post will prevent Burmillas from scratching furniture, carpets, and curtains.

A Burmilla needs a bed of its own, or it might decide your bed will do!

Feeding

An important part of caring for a Burmilla is providing quality food and fresh water every day. The food should be a blend of **protein**, vitamins, and minerals. This will give the cat the **nutrients** it needs to be healthy.

Most cats eat twice a day. Cats are often picky about what they eat, and will let their owners know what they prefer. Many cats like moist food. It comes in cans or pouches, and is often soft and chewy. It is close to what cats eat in the wild.

Dry food is another option. It is hard and crunchy. Many cats do not like dry food, but it can be helpful for cats with tooth problems. Sometimes, Burmillas have **tartar** that builds up on their teeth. Eating dry food helps clean the teeth.

It is important not to overfeed a cat.
An overweight cat can be unheaght.

Kittens

When a female Burmilla is close to a year old, she can begin to mate. After mating, a female is **pregnant** for about 65 days. When she delivers her **litter**, it is called kittening.

Newborn kittens are completely helpless. They cannot see or hear. They depend on their mother to care for them. They drink her milk and stay close to her to keep warm.

After 10 to 12 days, the kittens can see and hear. Their teeth begin to grow in. When they are three weeks old, they begin to explore their world.

For the first five weeks, kittens drink their mother's milk. Then, they are **weaned** onto solid food. The kittens spend their days learning and growing. They are able to leave their mother at 12 to 16 weeks old.

Burmillas have two to five kittens in an average litter.

Buying a Kitten

Have you decided the Burmilla is the right cat for your family? Burmillas are a rare **breed**, so finding one at a shelter is unlikely. So, you will need to find a good breeder.

Good breeders sell healthy, **socialized** cats that have had their **vaccines**. They also know the history of their cats. They will be able to suggest a kitten that is the right fit for your family.

When the kitten arrives at its new home, it may be scared or shy. It will need a few items right away. It will appreciate a quiet bed to rest in. Food and water and a **litter box** should be immediately available. Kittens are playful, so they will need toys! Most of all, kittens need lots of love and attention from their owners.

Kittens are very sociable
and spend most of their
time playing.

Glossary

blue - a coat color that is bluish gray.

breed - a group of animals sharing the same ancestors and appearance. A breeder is a person who raises animals. Raising animals is often called breeding them.

Cat Fanciers' Association - a group that sets the standards for judging all breeds of cats.

domestic - tame, especially relating to animals.

Felidae (FEHL-uh-dee) - the scientific Latin name for the cat family. Members of this family are called felids. They include lions, tigers, leopards, jaguars, cougars, wildcats, lynx, cheetahs, and domestic cats.

lilac - a coat color that is pinkish gray.

litter - all of the kittens born at one time to a mother cat.

litter box - a box filled with cat litter, which is similar to sand. Cats use litter boxes to bury their waste.

muzzle - an animal's nose and jaws.

neuter (NOO-tuhr) - to remove a male animal's reproductive glands.

nutrient - a substance found in food and used in the body. It promotes growth, maintenance, and repair.

pregnant - having one or more babies growing within the body.

protein - a substance which provides energy to the body and serves as a major class of foods for animals. Foods high in protein include cheese, eggs, fish, meat, and milk.

shed - to cast off hair, feathers, skin, or other coverings or parts by a natural process.

socialize - to adapt an animal to behaving properly around people or other animals in various settings.

spay - to remove a female animal's reproductive organs.

tartar - a hard, yellowish crust that forms on teeth when saliva acts on food particles.

tortoiseshell - a coat featuring patches of black, orange, and cream.

trait - a quality or feature of something.

tuft - a small bunch of feathered hair that grows close together.

undercoat - short hair or fur partly covered by longer protective fur.

vaccine (vak-SEEN) - a shot given to prevent illness or disease.

wean - to accustom an animal to eating food other than its mother's milk.

Websites

To learn more about Cats, visit **booklinks.abdopublishing.com**. These links are routinely monitored and updated to provide the most current information available.

Index

24